I TOLD YOU TO BUY CRYPTOCURRENCY!

This book is intended for entertainment purposes only. It does not provide financial, investment, legal, or professional advice. The author is not a financial advisor, and nothing in this book should be interpreted as financial guidance. Any decisions regarding cryptocurrency or investments are entirely your own and should be made with appropriate research and, when necessary, consultation with a qualified professional.

ISBN: 978-1-971419-43-5

Contact: Gbryellawhyt@gmail.com

I told you to buy Bitcoin
back in the day,

But you rolled your eyes
and walked away.

You said it was nonsense,
a digital joke,

Now I own a mansion—
you're still broke.

VVV

I staked VVV and
put
my AI on the payroll
—
it works around the
clock
while I just sit and
scroll.

My robot makes me
money while I'm
drinking by the pool.

You still have a
human boss... and
you called me the
fool.

You said, "INJ?
Another coin nobody can explain."

I loaded up anyway—
you said I was insane.

You bought yourself a speedboat
and cruised along the shore.

I bought a fucking submarine...
because boats felt poor.

You said, "NEAR?
Nobody talks about it—
that coin is fucking
dead."

I bought it while you
chased
another dog coin instead.

They built AI and chain
abstraction—
you still didn't care.

I made enough on NEAR
to buy a fucking polar
bear.

You said ETH was too
pricey
at a thousand a coin.

I bought it anyway—
you refused to join.

Now ETH bought my
grand piano;
I can't play a single song,

But when you're this
fucking rich,
being talented feels
wrong.

You said, "TAO?
AI crypto? Bro, that
sounds insane."

I bought a giant bag
and watched it melt
your brain.

You bought fancy
artwork
just to hang up and
boast.

I bought a haunted
mansion...
then kept the fucking
ghost.

I told you to buy SOL
at just eight a pop,

but you rolled your eyes
and told me to stop.

I know you must feel
like a tool,

so feel free to come over
and use my new pool.

I told you to buy XRP
back in the day,

but you rolled your eyes
and laughed it away.

You called it a scam,
said I'd lose every dime,

now the XRP Army and I
drink champagne all the
time.

I told you to buy DOGE
when it blew up on X,

you said, "A dog with a
coin?
What stupid shit comes
next?"

Then Elon tweeted once
and my DOGE went
insane,

now my Shiba has a
chauffeur—
and you still take the train.

Litecoin's an OG,
still holding its throne,

memecoins are mooning,
but I'm stacking my own.

"Wen Lambo?" they ask—
like they don't already
know,

I picked out the color
six years ago.

You said SUPER was stupid,
"Pixel pets? What a joke."

I loaded up on NFTs
while you stayed broke.

You said fake little animals
would never make me cash,

now I own a private safari—
and zebras eat my grass.

I went to Jupiter
to swap, now I'm
trading perps at night.

Then lending, staking,
limit orders—damn,
they got it right.

You said, "It's just
another DEX"—
I laughed and
bought the dip,

Now my girlfriend
thinks "Jupiter"
is where we park
the ship.

Kaspa's blockDAG
tech,
a true innovation.

GHOSTDAG protocol
—
a nerd's fascination.

You said, "That nerdy
shit
will never pay."

I bought a private
island...
with a fucking
runway.

I bought UNI, now I swap my crypto like a king,

liquidity pools do the work—I barely do a thing.

I even get a vote on what the protocol should do—

I bought myself a voice in DeFi... and still won't listen to you.

You said IMX was
stupid,
"Who buys shit inside a
game?"

I said, "Give
Immutable some time
—
you'll remember the
name."
I made so much money
off it, I was
feeling pretty slick,

So I bought the
homeless
brand-new tents—
to prove I'm not a dick.

You went all-in on
PEPE,
ETH gas fees a pain,

while I snagged WIF
on Solana—
low-cost, high gain.

WIF made me rich—
what else could I do?

Bought the Sphere...
and put my dog up, too.

On Base's runway,
AERO took flight,

I aped in early—
you said, "Yeah, right."

Made so much money
I bought the whole damn
team,

then built them a
stadium...
because rich people
dream.

Remember when you
mocked
my Chainlink play?

Said, "Oracles? Bro,
no one will pay."

Now I book first class
without hesitation,

while you're stuck at
work—
I'm always on
vacation!

I told you to buy
THETA,
you pushed it aside,

I loaded up my bags
and enjoyed the ride.

You stayed on
Coinbase,
said new apps were
a pain,

now you're still
broke—
while I'm on a
private plane.

"Don't buy that political shit!"
You laughed and called it trash.

So naturally I bought TRUMP—
and watched it print me cash.

You said politics and crypto
never mix—that made my day.

Then TRUMP paid off my G-Wagon—
150K.

You finally bought crypto
—BONK?
Bro, that was dumb.

I told you, "Skip this
fucking one"—
but you still bought
some.

A whale took over voting,
twenty million went
away.

You finally bought some
crypto...
on the worst fucking day.

You said, "XLM? Bro,
just use a bank."

Then paid a wire fee
while your transfer
fucking sank.

I sent mine round the
world before you
finished your call,

Now I'm drinking
in Saint-Tropez—
and your bank's still
"processing" it all.

You laughed when I
bought CHZ,
said, "Sports crypto?
That's weak."

You bought season
tickets—
I bought CHZ that
week.

Now you're spilling
nachos
in some shitty little
seat.
I'm drinking with the
owners—
with my feet up in the
suite.

You said, "BEAM?
Crypto gaming? Bro,
that shit's a joke."

Then spent five grand
on gaming gear
and somehow still went
broke.

You stayed up chasing
digital swords
and armor every night.

I made a fortune buying
BEAM—
you just learned how to
fight.

You said, "SUI? Another
Layer 1?
That shit is gonna tank."

I bought it while you
played it safe
and left your cash at the
bank.

You spent six months
researching,
afraid that you would
lose.

I made enough on SUI to
buy
a pool I'll never use.

You said PUMP was garbage, I said,
"Maybe, we'll see,"

Then that stupid little token started printing money for me.

I'm a philanthropist now,
so I had to give some more,

I bought the homeless new tent décor.

You said, "POPCAT?
It's a cat with its
mouth open wide."

I said, "Exactly,
genius"—then I
bought it on the side.

You spent months
doing research, trying
to pick the perfect bet.

I made money on a
cat...
you done overthinking
crypto yet?

You said, "AVAX?
Too risky, too steep."

I loaded up on AVAX
while you stayed
asleep.

It made me so rich,
I bought a ski resort
with a view.

I felt bad you missed
out...
so I'll let you ski there a
day or two.

You said, "ATOM?
Another blockchain?
Bro, that shit won't
fly."

I bought a giant bag
and watched that
bastard multiply.

You bought another
Rolex—I said, "Bro,
those are getting old."

I bought a fucking
meteorite...
apparently space
rocks come in gold.

BNB came from CZ—
yeah, he did time.

Pled guilty, four months—
the coin stayed in its prime.

You said, "After all that?
You're still buying?
You fool."

I bought a fucking kangaroo...
and taught it to DJ by the pool.

You said, "ONDO?
Real-world assets?
Sounds lame."

I bought a giant bag
and watched it change
the game.

You bought giant lawn
chess,
thought your setup was
sick.

I hired thirty-two
supermodels...
"Queen to c6!"

You said, "Render? AI tokens? Bro, give me a break."

I loaded up on RENDER just to prove your latest mistake.

I bought your dog Brian a ridiculously large bone.

I made so much on RENDER...
I had Brian cloned.

You said FET was
just dumb, so I
told you to wait.

Now AI agents do
my work while I
just celebrate.

You're still poor—
you just bought
BTC.

I made so much on
FET,
I built a snow
room for me.

You laughed when I bought PYTH, said, "That oracle is trash."

Then PYTH started moving and I made another stack of cash.

The homeless had their tents and mirrors—everything looked fine.

But what kind of philanthropist forgets the fucking wine?

You laughed at PENDLE while I traded future yield.

I bought YT and waited for the profits to be sealed.

My girlfriend said, "I need some space," while lying there in bed.

So I built her zero gravity—now she sleeps above my head.

You said FARTCOIN was stupid, just a joke somebody made,

I bought a giant bag of it and watched the joke get paid.

My girlfriend said, "This crypto thing is nothing but hot air,"

So I built a private wind tunnel just to blow around her hair.

You liked PENGU too,
but bought a baby-sized
amount,

I loaded up on PENGU
—
now there are commas
in my account.

My girlfriend likes
penguins,
what can I say?

I give her a Birkin bag
and a PENGU every
day.

You said CRV was boring,
"Stablecoins? Who gives a shit?"

I threw my money in the pool
and made a fortune from it.

My girlfriend said, "Less crypto,
more time with me, honey."

So I bought her another diamond...
and went back to making money.

You laughed at my crypto,
said I'd lose every dime,

Turns out being wrong
gets expensive over time.

I got the mansion, the yacht,
the hot wife and the jet,

You got one thing I don't have!

Don't forget.

www.ingramcontent.com/pod-product-compliance
Lightning Source LLC
LaVergne TN
LVHW070626061126
851857LV00002B/17
9781971419435